D0638731

To

From

Chicken Soup for the College Soul™

Copyright © 1999 Jack Canfield
and Mark Victor Hansen

Published by Blessings Unlimited
Pentagon Towers, P.O. Box 398004
Edina, MN 55439

Design by Lecy Design

All rights reserved. No part of this book may be
reproduced in any form without permission
in writing from the publisher.

ISBN 1-58375-615-9

A *Little Spoonful* of

Chicken Soup for the COLLEGE Soul™

College Talk

$\mathcal{I}$t seemed to come on like the flu. Suddenly, out of nowhere, everyone was talking about college. Lunchtime discussions changed from who's dating whom into who's going to what college and who did or did not get accepted. And just like the flu leaves its victims feeling awful and helpless, such was the case for this new fascinating subject and me.

I don't clearly remember the actual conversations. I do, however, remember why I wasn't interested in all this "college talk." We didn't have enough money for me to go to a real college. I would begin my college years at a junior college. This was the final word and I had accepted it. I didn't even mind terribly. I just wished everyone would stop talking about this university and that Ivy League school.

The truth is, I was jealous. I had worked so hard to get good grades in school and for what? Each time I found out someone else I knew had just been accepted to the college of their dreams I would turn a deeper shade of green. I didn't like feeling this way, but I couldn't help it. I felt like they were going to jump ahead of me. They were going to have the big life experiences that turn a teenager into an adult and I was going to get left behind.

My boyfriend was very sweet and barely mentioned it every time an envelope arrived for him with a "Congratulations, you've been accepted to yet another college of your choice!" I knew about them only because his parents lacked the sensitivity with which he was so blessed. He always shrugged it off and would tell me, "You would have had the same response. Watch, you'll get a full scholarship to the college of your choice in two years and you can laugh at us all for foolishly killing ourselves to arrive at the same place." He had a point. I just thought it was awfully sweet of him to make sure I saw it this way.

My friends and I kept in touch those first few months and more often than not, I was the one offering words of support and understanding. They spoke of roommates from hell, classes they couldn't get into, and the ones they did being so big they couldn't even see their professor. Not only could I see mine, but one of my favorites invited us to his house on a lake. We would go there for class and stay hours afterwards talking and sharing our theories on human behavior. It was because of this class that I decided to major in psychology.

Needless to say, my tortured thoughts of being left behind while they went out and gathered life experiences in huge doses changed to thoughts of counting my blessings. I was getting a fine serving of life experiences. I was letting go of friends and my first true love. I was moving into a humble abode that for the first time in my life I could call my own and I was taking a full load of classes by choice, not requirement.

As time passed and I grew more and more comfortable with my circumstances, I was also able to understand something I hadn't when I was angry and envious. Real life will be filled with moments of friends making more or loved ones being promoted first. When these things happen, I know I will be prepared. I have already had a taste of this experience and I passed the test quite nicely.

KIMBERLY KIRBERGER

Hani

The day I met Hani Irmawati, she was a shy, seventeen-year-old girl standing alone in the parking lot of the international school in Indonesia, where I teach English. The school is expensive and does not permit Indonesian students to enroll. She walked up to me and asked if I could help her improve her English. I could tell it took immense courage for the young Indonesian girl in worn clothing to approach me and ask for my help.

"Why do you want to improve your English?" I asked her, fully expecting her to talk about finding a job in a local hotel.

"I want to go to an American university,"

she said with quiet confidence. Her idealistic dream made me want to cry.

I agreed to work with her after school each day on a volunteer basis. For the next several months, Hani woke each morning at five and caught the city bus to her public high school. During the one-hour ride, she studied for her regular classes and prepared the English lessons I had given her the day before. At four o'clock in the afternoon, she arrived at my classroom, exhausted but ready to work. With each passing day, as Hani struggled with college-level English, I grew more fond of her. She worked harder than most of my wealthy expatriate students.

Hani lived in a two-room house with her parents and two brothers. Her father was a building custodian and her mother was a maid. When I went to their neighborhood to meet them, I learned that their combined yearly income was 750 U.S. dollars. It wasn't enough to meet the expenses of even one month in an American university. Hani's enthusiasm was increasing with her language ability, but I was becoming more and more discouraged.

One morning in December 1998, I received the announcement of a scholarship opportunity for a major American university. I excitedly tore open the envelope and studied the requirements, but it wasn't long before I dropped the form in despair. There was just no way, I thought, for Hani to meet these qualifications. She had never led a club or an organization, because in her school these things simply did not exist. She had no guidance counselor and no impressive standardized test scores, because there were no such tests for her to take.

She did, however, have more determination than any student I'd ever seen. When Hani came into the classroom that day, I told her of the scholarship. I also told her that I believed there was no way for her to apply. I encouraged her to be, as I put it, "realistic" about her future and not to plan so strongly on coming to America. Even after my somber lecture, Hani remained steadfast.

"Will you send in my name?" she asked.

I didn't have the heart to turn her down. I completed the application, filling in each blank with the painful truth about her academic life, but also with my praise of her courage and her perseverance. I sealed up the envelope and told Hani her chances for acceptance ranged somewhere between slim and none.

In the weeks that followed, Hani increased her study of English, and I arranged for her to take the Test of English Fluency in Jakarta. The entire computerized test would be an enormous challenge for someone who had never before touched a computer. For two weeks, we studied computer parts and how they worked. Then, just before Hani went to Jakarta, she received a letter from the scholarship association. *What a cruel time for the rejection to arrive*, I thought. Trying to prepare her for disappointment, I opened the letter and began to read it to her. She had been accepted.

I leaped about the room ecstatically, shocked. Hani stood by, smiling quietly, but almost certainly bewildered by my surprise. The image of her face in that moment came back to me time and time again in the following week. I finally realized that it was I who had learned something Hani had known from the beginning: It is not intelligence alone that brings success, but also the drive to succeed,

the commitment to work hard and the courage
to believe in yourself.

JAMIE WINSHIP

*Reach for the sky because if you
should happen to miss, you'll still be
among the stars.*

ROSA TORCASIO

Your Legacy

I had a philosophy professor who was the quintessential eccentric philosopher. His disheveled appearance was highlighted by a well-worn tweed sport coat and poor-fitting thick glasses, which often rested on the tip of his nose. Every now and then, as most philosophy professors do, he would go off on one of those esoteric and existential "what's the meaning of life" discussions. Many of those discussions went nowhere, but there were a few that really hit home. This was one of them:

"Respond to the following questions by a show of hands," my professor instructed.

"How many of you can tell me something about your parents?" Everyone's hand went up.

"How many of you can tell me something about your grandparents?" About three-fourths of the class raised their hands.

"How many of you can tell me something about your great-grandparents?" Two out of the sixty students raised their hands.

"Look around the room," he said. "In just two short generations hardly any of us even know who our own great-grandparents were. Oh sure, maybe we have an old, tattered photograph tucked away in a musty cigar box or know the classic family story about how one of them walked five miles to school barefoot. But how many of us really know who they were, what they thought, what they were proud of, what they were afraid of, or what they dreamed about? Think about that. Within three generations our ancestors are all but forgotten. Will this happen to you?

"Here's a better question. Look ahead three generations. You are long gone. Instead of you sitting in this room, now it's your great-grandchildren. What will they have to say about you? Will they know about you? Or will you be forgotten, too?

"Is your life going to be a warning or an example? What legacy will you leave? The choice is yours. Class dismissed."

Nobody rose from their seat for a good five minutes.

TONY D'ANGELO

Learning How to Be Roommates

I was never very neat. Later in life I learned to attribute this flaw to my creative genius, saying that my bouts of disorganization were simply the flip side of my unique gifts and talents. Yet, when I arrived at college, I hadn't come up with any impressive reasons for my big messes. They just *were*—and my roommate didn't seem to appreciate their contribution to my bright future.

I'm not sure why they stuck us together. I don't think they could have possibly picked two more different people to room together. Kim was extremely organized. She labeled everything and each item she owned had its place. She even had one of those cute little pencil holders—and used it! Mine had become a collection spot for bits and pieces of paper, odds and ends. I think one pen may have found its way into the pencil holder but I certainly didn't put it there.

Kim and I fed off each other. She got neater and I got messier. She would complain about my dirty clothes, I would complain about Lysol headaches. She would nudge my clothing over to one side and I would lay one of my books on her uncluttered desk.

It came to a head one fateful October evening. Kim came into the room and had some kind of fit because one of my shoes had

found its way (inexplicably) beneath her bed.
I don't know what was so significant about
that shoe but it infuriated her! She picked it
up, tossed it toward my side of the room and
managed to knock my lamp onto the floor.
The light bulb shattered, covering the layer
of clothes I had been planning to fold that
very night. I leapt off the bed in horror and
immediately started yelling about her insensitivity
and rudeness. She yelled back similar frustrations
and we each ended up pushing toward the door
to be the first to slam our way out of the room.

I'm sure we wouldn't have lasted a day
or two longer in that room. Probably not even
a night, if it hadn't been for the phone call she

received. I was sitting on my bed, fuming. She was sitting on hers, fuming.... I don't even know why we had both returned to each other's company.

When the phone rang she picked it up and I could tell right away it wasn't good news. I knew Kim had a boyfriend back home and I could tell from her end of the conversation that he was breaking up with her. Though I didn't mean for it to happen, I could feel the warm feelings of empathy rising up in my heart. Losing a boyfriend was something no girl should go through alone.

I sat up in my bed. Kim wouldn't look at me and when she hung up the phone she quickly crawled under her covers and I could hear her quiet sobbing. What to do? I didn't want to just walk over (I was still a little miffed) but I didn't want to leave her either. I smiled as I got the idea.

Slowly, I began to clear up my side of the room. I took back the book I had set on her desk and I cleaned up the socks and the shirts. I put some pencils in my pencil holder and made my bed. I straightened the dresser top (but not the drawers—I had my limits!) and swept the floor, even on her side. I got so into my work that I didn't even notice that Kim had come out from under the covers. She was watching my every move, her tears dried and her expression one of disbelief. When I was finally done I went and sat on the end of her bed. Not really saying anything but just sitting. I guess I didn't know what to say. Her hand was warm. I thought it would be cold, probably because I always thought the organized were pretty heartless. But no. Her hand was warm as it reached over to grasp mine. I looked up into Kim's eyes and she smiled at me. "Thanks."

Kim and I stayed roommates for the rest of that year. We didn't always see eye to eye, but we learned the key to living together. Giving in, cleaning up and holding on.

Elsa Lynch

It is not intelligence alone that brings success, but also the drive to succeed, the commitment to work hard and the courage to believe in yourself.

JAMIE WINSHIP

Knowing Where to Tap

*B*efore setting off to college, my father sat me down and shared this memorable story with me. It is one I shall never forget. My father is not college educated, yet he possesses more wisdom and insight than most college professors I have met. After you read this story, you'll know what I mean.

There is an old story of a boilermaker who was hired to fix a huge steamship boiler system that was not working well. After listening to the engineer's description of the problems and asking a few questions, he went to the boiler room. He looked at the maze of twisting pipes, listened to the thump of the boiler and the hiss of escaping steam for a few minutes, and felt some pipes with his hands. Then he hummed softly to himself, reached into his overalls and took out a small hammer, and tapped a bright red valve one time. Immediately, the entire system began working perfectly, and the boilermaker went home. When the steamship owner received a bill for one thousand dollars, he complained that the boilermaker had only been in the engine room for fifteen minutes and requested an itemized bill. So the boilermaker sent him a bill that reads as follows:

For tapping the valve:	$ .50
For knowing where to tap:	$ 999.50
TOTAL:	$ 1,000.00

"Tony," he said, "I want you to go to
college so that you can get your degree, but
more important, I want you to return with
an education."

TONY D'ANGELO

The world of tomorrow belongs to the

person who has the vision today.

ROBERT SCHULLER

The Rest of
the Story

Jennifer would have caught my attention even if she hadn't stopped to talk that afternoon. The first couple of weeks in my writing class are always a bit unsettling. The students are a blur of unfamiliar faces, most of them freshmen trying to acclimate themselves to their new environment. When Jennifer approached me with a question after the second day, I was grateful for the chance to connect at least one name with a face.

Her writing wasn't perfect, but her effort was. She worked hard and pushed herself to excel. She was excited to learn, which made me enjoy teaching her. I didn't realize then how much she would also teach me.

One Friday afternoon, a few weeks into the semester, Jennifer stopped by after class. She wasn't clarifying an assignment or asking a question about a paper I'd returned.

"I didn't make it to career day yesterday," she said quietly. "I was at the health center the whole day." I gave her a sideways look, startled. "I'm fine now," she reassured me with confidence. "It was just a virus." Then she was gone.

Two nights later, her father called to tell me that Jennifer would be missing a few classes. She had been hospitalized with meningitis. I heard from him again a few days later, and again after that. Her condition had worsened, he said, and it appeared she might not finish the semester at all.

Jenny remained hospitalized, ninety miles away from home. Her mother stayed by her side, camped out in the corner of a cramped hospital room, sleeping night after night on a chair. In the middle of the night, while Jenny slept, her mother sneaked out—but just to duck down the hall for a quick shower.

Grandparents, ministers and long-standing friends all made their pilgrimages to the hospital room. Jenny's condition grew worse, not better. I was terrified when I saw the pail, emaciated girl who had only ten days earlier radiated life and warmth in my classroom. When her grandparents arrived, she spoke the only words during our visit. "This is my college writing teacher," she announced proudly, in a tiny voice. I remembered what her father had said in his first phone call: "School means everything to Jenny."

A week later, Jenny herself called me to tell me she was on the road to recovery. "I'll be back," she insisted. "I have no doubt," I told her, choking back tears. But around the same time, news reports announced the meningitis-induced death of another student at another school. Jenny sank back into her hospital bed.

Then, five weeks later, I walked into my classroom to find Jenny in her seat, smiling as she talked to the students around her. I caught my breath as her rail-thin body approached my desk, and she handed over all of her missed assignments, completed with thought and excellence. The strength of her will to overcome shone out of her pale, weak, eighteen-year-old face. It would be a few more days, though, before I learned the rest of the story.

Jenny's suitemates, Maren and Kate, were just getting up the Sunday morning that Jenny was dragging herself into the bathroom they shared. She had a horrendous headache and had been throwing up all night. Forty-five minutes later, as the two were leaving for church, she was still there. Maren had a bad feeling about Jenny and asked her Sunday school class to pray for her. When they returned to the dorm three hours later, Jenny was still violently ill. Concerned that she was becoming dehydrated, they decided to take her to the emergency room.

The two girls lifted Jenny up and carried her out to the car, then from the car to the hospital. They spent the next seven hours at their friend's side, tracking down her parents, responding to doctors and trying to comfort a very sick eighteen-year-old through a CAT scan, a spinal tap and myriad other medical tests. They left the hospital when Jenny's parents arrived but were back the next morning when the doctors confirmed that the meningitis was bacterial. By noon, they had the whole two-hundred-member campus Christian group praying for Jenny.

I credit these two young students with the miracle of Jenny's life. That same semester, just an hour away on another college campus, two students found a friend in a similar condition—motionless and deathly ill. Instead of getting him to a hospital, they took a permanent marker and wrote on his forehead the number of shots he had consumed in celebration of his twenty-first birthday. Their friend died of alcohol poisoning. Jenny finished the semester with a 4.0.

I remember being asked as a college freshman who I considered a hero. I didn't have an answer then. Since that time, I've learned that I may have been looking for heroes in the wrong places. Ask me now who I admire, and I'll tell you about a couple of ordinary college students I know.

Jo Wiley Cornell

I Passed
the Test

T was just eighteen years old when I entered nursing school, easily the youngest member of my class. Consequently, I was the subject of a great deal of teasing and good-natured ribbing from my classmates, many of whom were single mothers and older women returning to school for a second career.

Unfortunately, I became ill one week and missed a crucial test on the subject of mental health. This was particularly important to me since I planned to enter the mental-health field once I became a full-fledged nurse. Being a serious student, I immediately scheduled a time to re-test and began cramming for this exam.

My fellow classmates knew how important this exam was to me and encouraged me as much as possible.

On the day of my test, as scheduled, I came to the classroom an hour early where one of my instructors administered the test. It was indeed a difficult exam, with more than one hundred questions pertaining to brain development and the latest trends in mental health. My intense study sessions served me well and, in less than forty minutes, I passed the test with flying colors.

Anxious to share my test results with my fellow students, I ran to the hospital coffee shop where we students spent our free time with members of the hospital support staff. As soon as I entered the coffee shop, I cried out in a loud voice, "I passed my mental retardation test!"

As I looked around the busy coffee shop, I could not find any of my classmates. Instead, a group of maintenance men, with confused looks on their faces, rose to give me a standing ovation.

PAULA LOPEZ-CRESPIN

Our Community

One Tuesday evening in the beginning of the fall 1996 semester at Shippensburg University, sirens sounded. These sirens were not in celebration; they were a cry to the university that something was wrong. A house, only one block away, was on fire. Nine of the university's students lived there.

From the minute the word got out that help was needed, it seemed like everyone showed up. The victims of the fire were offered endless invitations for housing for the night. The very next day, everyone got into gear to do their part in helping them. Flyers were posted with items that were immediately needed, just to get these students through this next couple of days. Boxes for donations and money jars were placed in every residence hall.

As a residence director, I went before the students in my hall to ask them to do what they could. I knew that college students don't have much, but I asked them to do their best: "Every little bit will help." I really didn't think they could do much. I was proved wrong.

At the hall council meeting the night after the fire, my residents decided to have a wing competition, where each wing of the building would team up to see who could bring in the most donations. I announced that the wing that won would receive a free pizza party.

Thursday evening we announced over the PA system that we were beginning the wing competition. Within minutes, the place exploded. The single large box that I had placed in the lobby was overflowing. We quickly grabbed more boxes, and we watched in amazement as they, too, filled to the brim. Members of the resident assistant staff and I began to count the items. I was astonished by what I saw, and I was inspired by these kids.

When we came to the final tally, the winners turned to me and announced that they would like to donate their winnings as well. They wanted the victims of the fire to have their pizza party.

Tears welled up in my eyes. I had watched these students jump to action, work tirelessly and donate all that they could. And then, as if that were not enough, they handed over their reward. I was touched and so very proud of them.

CHRISTA F. SANDELIER

Cherish your visions and your dreams,

as they are the children of your soul

and the blueprints of

your ultimate achievements.

NAPOLEON HILL

My Sanctuary

$\mathscr{I}$t is three in the morning on a Tuesday, and I'm walking toward table eighteen, the one I call home. I pass the waiters, give a brief nod to the regulars and take my seat. I order the "usual," water and peanut butter pie. Yes, I'm at an all-night diner.

I start to take out my books, knowing full well that I will be stuck on the same page of Socrates that I've been on for the better part of the semester. Of course, it's early—for my group that is. I wait for the empty chairs around me to be filled.

Just as the Muzak songs start to repeat themselves, Shana and Jenny walk in. I am greeted with the usual big hugs and smiles. Suddenly, the diner stops being a twenty-four-hour restaurant with bad service and becomes my place—my home away from the prison-like confines of my drab cell, a.k.a. my dorm room. For the next couple of hours, we will joke about people we know, talk about books, muse on the meaning of life, quote movies and create new private jokes. Table number eighteen is our inner sanctum.

During my senior year of college, I started going to the diner for a reprieve from a dorm room that felt like it was closing in on me. Not to mention the phones, the stereo and the computer. How could anyone seriously expect to have good study habits? Some friends of mine told me about the place; they went there to study, and they really liked it.

So I tried it. It felt remarkably freeing. I started going there every night (except weekends, of course), and, believe me it was not because the pies were that great either. Maybe it would force me to pry open my books, and my grades would improve. Right? Well…

But that's not the point. I mean, anyone who has gone to college knows that it's not only forcing yourself to wake up at 7:45 A.M. (after you had gone to sleep two hours earlier) to listen to a professor spoon-feeding you information regarding the significance of the Battle of

Hastings. It is also about finding a little haven where you can create what will be the most important thing in your life—yourself. At a school of thirty-five thousand people, I found a small place that was as familiar to me as my Social Security number.

That place was the diner. It was where advice on dating and anything else flowed freely. Where we would get nutty with exhaustion and no one minded. There was a time I spilled water all over myself, and we laughed until we cried. There were the victory laps over acing exams.

Through laughter, tears, learning, growing and the occasional free ice cream,

we found a sanctuary. A place where we could
be ourselves.

ERIC LINDER

The highest reward for a person's

toil is not what they get for it,

but what they become by it.

JOHN RUSHKIN

A Better Message

My senior year of high school, I wanted to be a social worker like my older sister, Lynn. She had really inspired me. I wanted to help people, to make a difference in their lives, just like she was doing.

I knew I had work to do because I hadn't really applied myself in high school. It was more social for me than anything else. But I was looking ahead to my future, and I knew that if I really wanted to do this, I was going to need help. I made an appointment to see a guidance counselor, Mr. Shaw.

He listened to my inspired rap as I went on and on about the wonders of a helping career.

I could actually help make a difference in the world! Mr. Shaw looked back at me in disbelief. "You're not college material," he said clearly and deliberately. It felt like my heart stopped... frozen in the moment of those icy words.

That evening I broke the news to my parents. Seeing how distraught I was, and how sincere I was in really wanting to go to college, they offered to help. They found a small college that would take me if I could manage to get a C average out of the current semester. It was too late. I had goofed around too much, and even my best efforts could not bring up my grade-point average.

My parents were so wonderful and supportive. They found another small college whose financial status would permit anyone to attend. In other words, they would take anyone with a pulse. I felt like such a loser. Mr. Shaw's resounding words came back to me: "You're not college material." And I was beginning to believe it. So much so that I was flunking out—even at this college.

I gave up. I believed Mr. Shaw was right about me. After I left college, I moved home again and started working part-time jobs. Maybe college wasn't for me. But deep down in my heart I knew that I truly wanted to be a teacher or social worker, and...that would require a college degree. No getting around it.

What would I do? I simply had to try again, I had to believe in myself even if no one else did. With all the courage I could muster, I enrolled in a community college nearby and took one course in their night school. I was shocked when I received my grade. I got an A. Maybe it was a mistake or some sort of fluke. I took another course and earned another A. Wow.

I made an appointment to see one of my professors. Things were turning around, and I needed guidance. Dr. Sarah Cohen, my professor in child psychology, told me to relax and enjoy my experience; I was doing very well by all standards. She also said that I was fun, bright and could do anything I put my mind to. Here was an educational expert with a different message. I felt empowered. I was on my way.

I graduated from that community college with honors and went on to earn my B.A. in psychology and my M.A. in psychology from New York University. The very same degree the illustrious Mr. Shaw holds. I felt vindicated.

I realized that choosing who you believe in can change your life. When I believed in Mr. Shaw my life fell apart and there was no way I would ever realize my dream. But when I believed in myself and persevered through seemingly insurmountable odds, I encountered more people who inspired and supported me the way Dr. Cohen had.

As Henry Ford once said, "If you think you can, or if you think you can't…you're right."

CAROL GRACE ANDERSON

Do not wish to be anything but what you are, and try to be that perfectly.

SAINT FRANCIS DeSALES